ALEXANDRA HILLER

UNTANGLED

Navigating the hot mess of grief and finding life

Copyright © 2023 Alexandra Hiller

The moral rights of the author have been asserted. This book is copyright. Apart from any fair dealing for the purpose of private study, research, criticism or review, as permitted under the Copyright Act, no part may be reproduced or transmitted in any form or by any means electronic or mechanical, including photocopying and recording, without prior written permission from the author.

For all enquiries, including permission requests, write to:
lexhiller@gmail.com

ISBN: 978-0-6454095-3-6

Published by Diamond Stories Collection Pty Ltd
www.diamondstories.au

Cover design by Karen Wallis, Taloula Press
www.taloulapress.com

Text design and typeset by David Bradbury
www.dbtype.com.au

Cataloguing-in-Publication details are available from the National Library of Australia
www.trove.nla.gov.au

Printed and bound in Australia by PRINTBOOKS

The paper in this book is PEFC certified.

'Alexandra takes readers on an honest but beautifully crafted journey into the realms of grief and recovery and doesn't shy away from feelings of shame, regret and hurt. She allows you to contemplate your own grieving process while wrapping you in a warm hug. Heartbreaking but utterly compelling, it's hard to put down.'
Jeannie Vandervelde

'Although I didn't think my emotions could handle it, I read *Untangled* in one sitting, riding the waves of tears and laughter through Alexandra's story. She describes grief as a hot mess – and indeed it is! Thank you for giving me permission to cry, wail and to be as messy as I need to be.'
Jez Olivero

'Alexandra's story is a deeply personal insight into how devastating the process of grief can be. This book is raw, vulnerable and incredibly generous, and I know that everyone who reads this will benefit, as we all, at some time in our life, will experience the pain and loss and grief of being human.'
Karina Smith

'*Untangled* is a raw and courageous story of learning to survive the tornado of grief. It is inspiring to all who have found themselves on the same journey as I too found myself when I lost my parents months apart when I was a teenager. I thought that grief was meant to be "dealt" with then put away forever. Alexandra reminded me that grief is personal and to allow my own experience.'
Michelle Wilden

'*Untangled* offers a message of optimism, compassion and the transformational power of self-awareness, reminding us that it's never too late to disentangle the emotional tangles of our past and find our real selves. It's a tale of valour, tenacity and the significance of accepting oneself. Alexandra conveys a message of self-love and the value of personal development.'
Kateryna Lavrynenko

'In our Western culture, to talk of death and grief is somewhat taboo and mostly awkward. This book felt like a solid best friend who knew what to say and what stories to share in a dark time. *Untangled* offers honesty and support in one's own complex, messy and often lonely journey through losing someone you love.'
Eve Kermack

'Despite her journey through complex grief, Alexandra shines a guiding light for others experiencing heartbreaking loss.'
Rosemary Connors

DEDICATION

To Stuart Ralph Speed.

A darling man and gentle soul
who became a most powerful teacher.

'In the midst of winter, I found there was, within me, an invincible summer.'

Albert Camus

CONTENTS

	Introduction / ix
CHAPTER 1	The beginning of the end / 1
CHAPTER 2	The actual beginning – a happy tale / 9
CHAPTER 3	Hospital / 15
CHAPTER 4	The aftermath / 23
CHAPTER 5	Back to hospitality / 28
CHAPTER 6	Nine months later / 33
CHAPTER 7	Japan / 36
CHAPTER 8	Berlin Part 1 / 50
CHAPTER 9	Berlin Part 2 / 58
CHAPTER 10	New York / 67
CHAPTER 11	Untangling / 73
CHAPTER 12	Final musings / 79
	Acknowledgements / 82
	About the author / 84

INTRODUCTION

My dear friend,

I'm so sorry to hear that you are grieving.

It is such an intense and painful place to be in and I know that words can be so frustratingly ineffectual at this time. But even though I've just said that, I still want to offer you my words of comfort.

I want to share with you my own rather messy story, not to take away from your experience, but in the hope that you might gain a shred of comfort from knowing that you are not alone and there is someone else out there who has untangled this hot mess of grief too.

UNTANGLED

    I thank you in advance for holding this space for me while I share what took place almost 17 years ago. The time when my partner died and my world changed. It's all still here, fully preserved, just biding its time to be given a voice. I hope that in reading my story, you will find some compassion and kindness for yourself along the way as I have for myself too.

x

CHAPTER 1

The beginning of the end

I remember seeing Stuart's jaundiced face in the sunlight for the first time and I knew something was really wrong.

We had been living in North Melbourne, for only a couple of months, after making the reluctant move from the vibrant, bar-filled Fitzroy. Stuart loved Fitzroy. He always said that we were Fitzroyalty, which was certainly true for him, but I always felt uncomfortable claiming that title.

Stuart belonged to a golden era of Melbourne musicians. He was well known and well loved and had lived a charmed life. He had played all over the world, played with amazing musi-

UNTANGLED

cians and knew his way around a beverage or two.

When I got a look into the world of musicians, it was scary to see how much booze was given to them. After each gig, venues would give the musos what are called 'band riders', which consist of copious bottles of spirits, wine, beer. Whatever they want, depending on how famous the band is. Stuart would often come home with a bottle of some kind of booze in his bag. He would even top up his water bottle with gin or vodka from the band rider. I never knew that until my lovely friend Emma took a swig of 'water' from his bottle and spat it out all over me, burning my eyes.

People would always buy Stu a drink when we went out and he had his pubs and bars all lined up. He had a system in place. Everyone buying him a drink, me included, thought he was having his first drink of the night with them. Then he'd move on to the next venue to do it all again. When we moved to North Melbourne, Stuart was in a panic and I had no idea why he was so upset about the move. I knew something wasn't right, but I didn't have all the pieces to see things clearly. It turned out he was distressed as he didn't have his drinking structure set up in our new suburb. I had no idea about the extent of his pain or his illness.

We had to move as we were evicted from our Fitzroy

THE BEGINNING OF THE END

abode for being really far behind in rent. They never told us; we just had a phone call from the real estate people to see when a good time was to come over and show some prospective tenants the house!

I was the only breadwinner and had been for the last couple of years of our relationship, and let me tell you that it wasn't that much bread! I had transitioned from working in one of Melbourne's most vibrant restaurants, MoMo, by Greg Malouf, into the event-theming industry, working as a stylist. This felt a necessary transition to me as I could have some creative expression and feel more like an artist even if I was working for someone else. My pay had taken a huge hit. No more tips from hospitality to bump it up each week. Stu's excuse for not working was that the music had died. He wasn't being hired as there was no work, not like the old days. In hindsight, I think it was because he had become unreliable because of his drinking.

We had been in North Melbourne for about three months and Stuart wasn't paying rent. I was already feeling burnt out and exhausted from trying to support us both financially and emotionally. I would try and inspire him to find a new take on music and find his own path as the old path was not working anymore, but he wasn't listening and it was draining. I loved him but I couldn't live with him anymore. I asked him to go back and

UNTANGLED

stay with his father for a while. We would have long chats about this – it was me talking and he would just look at me and then go up to the bedroom to take in what I had just said. In reality, it was him going up to get a drink to numb everything, to numb the rejection. I always felt that by asking him to leave, albeit temporarily, I had driven the last nail in the coffin. That I was the one who pushed him over the edge to drink more.

In all of this mess, I never ever thought that death was an option. I always thought we would transcend any issues like people in relationships are meant to. But I never had the complete picture. Stuart was really good at keeping me in the dark. It wasn't until he died that people started coming forward with their stories and I started to see what had been going on. Ironic isn't it, that sometimes you have to wait till death to find out the truth about someone?

It's confronting seeing that truth after they've gone. There was such a moment for me when I had to find a suit of Stuart's for him to wear in the coffin. It was a strange task to be doing, choosing what someone else should wear. It felt somehow invasive, imposing my choice on him, and as I opened his wardrobe door I felt even more like a trespasser. This was his private space. With each layer removed from the enormous pile of clothes, like the layers of an onion, those feelings began

THE BEGINNING OF THE END

to dissipate and were replaced by anger and shock. Instead of touching soft fabrics, my hands found the hard surface of glass from the numerous vodka bottles hidden at the very bottom. I felt sick! The sense of betrayal was intense. It was like finding out he had been having an affair all along. I felt as though I had been living a lie and it was devastating.

I realise now that in the last few weeks before he went into hospital that I was seeing him only at night time. I was setting up events during the day and wouldn't be home until late evening. I felt that a huge chasm had opened up between us and we both didn't know how to cross it anymore. He was avoiding me as he didn't want to have any more conversations about finding work or moving out. I was avoiding him because I didn't know how to fix the situation, I didn't know how to fix him, I didn't know how to fix us. I felt that I had lost the charming, vibrant Stuart. He had lost his passion for life and I didn't know how to help him get it back.

That morning when I first saw his jaundice, I was running late for work. I had to ask Stu for a lift because my car was getting fixed. As we got in his car I looked over and saw him in the sunlight for the first time in many weeks. His skin and eyes were a turmeric yellow! It chilled me to my core. I burst into floods of tears and wailed at him to go to the doctors. Something was incredibly wrong.

Later that day I got a call from him. He sounded high and a bit crazy. He was saying how wonderful the doctors were and how everyone had been so lovely to him, and that I didn't need to worry anymore as he was staying in hospital for a few nights. A huge wave of relief washed over me. Finally, he was going to be looked after and supported in hospital. He was going to get the help he needed, get stronger and start afresh.

When I did go to see him in the hospital a few days later, one of the doctors pulled me aside and told me what had happened that day. Stuart had gone to a GP, and the doctor had taken one look at him and told him to get to emergency immediately! Which Stuart did, but not before going to a bar to top up with Dutch courage, and when at emergency, blew an alcohol reading off the charts! The doctor didn't tell me much more other than Stuart shouldn't drink and that his drinking might be more serious than I thought.

My conversation with the doctor left me shaken. I felt it was unknown ground I was walking upon. It felt murky, uncertain and there was a seriousness there that I didn't understand. I looked in on Stuart and found him sleeping peacefully, oblivious to my personal turmoil. As I sat down beside his bed, I noticed that he had stashed his brown leather bag that he took everywhere

THE BEGINNING OF THE END

with him underneath. That dark murkiness came bubbling up again, urging me to look in his bag. I think I already knew what I would find in there as I pulled out a scrunched brown paper wrapper with a whiskey bottle inside.

I was so mad at him that he would do this to himself. He was meant to be in hospital getting better, not indulging his drinking. He was meant to be safe. I grabbed him by the shoulders and shook him awake. He stared at me, bleary eyed and confused, as I thrust the whiskey bottle in his face. 'What the fuck are you doing this for? Just stop it! STOP IT!' I said before bursting into tears. It was actually quite dramatic as I then stormed out of the hospital, clutching the whiskey bottle, with mascara running down my face.

It was all very surreal. It felt like we were in some weird limbo. Then we got the call from the hospital that we were to have a family meeting with the doctors. The morning of the meeting, as I was getting ready, I broke down. I was on the floor of the shower in a foetal position, crying uncontrollably. I felt bereft as all the fear, uncertainty and murkiness overwhelmed me. I could feel that something big was coming.

I met Stuart's dad, brother, sister and her husband in the foyer of the hospital. There was a brittleness and nervousness to us all that morning as we all knew something serious was in the air. None of us wanted to acknowledge it as we chatted and spoke in pleasantries, avoiding each other's eyes. As we headed upstairs, the nervousness changed to an undercurrent of fear. The deep sadness within all of us was tangible as we filed into the meeting room. This is when we found out the truth. The head doctor told us that Stuart had scarred his liver so badly that it couldn't regenerate. He was operating on only 1% of his liver, his kidneys were failing, and his situation would most likely be terminal!

It felt like hours before the doctor spoke again. It was as though his words were floating above me. 'We have a new drug we'd like to try that might help kickstart the kidneys.' At the word 'help' I was fully alert. My body buzzed. There was hope. Maybe he will be the one to defy the odds and get through this. Maybe he will get better after all. I was deliriously convinced that he would.

CHAPTER 2

The actual beginning – a happy tale

I met darling Stuart in the early 2000s in the heart of Fitzroy on a cold Melbourne winter's night.

Every Sunday, my friends and I would go to a pumping Latino night at the Night Cat. It was a cavernous space with clusters of intimate lounge spaces for lovers to cosy up in and a big central bar for the booze hounds to hang off. Back then I thought it was super cool Melbourne chic!

Right in the middle of the space was a collection of

UNTANGLED

amazing musicians called Los Cabrones. They were, and probably still are, an incredible Afro-Cuban Latin-jazz group. Around 15 of them playing horns, percussion and more. So visually wild!

The place would be packed with sweaty, writhing bodies dancing and surrounding the band. It was the sheer joy of music and dancing. No judgement from anyone. Everyone from anywhere was welcome and accepted.

Earlier that winter's day, I had shown one of my commissioned paintings to a client and they loved it. It was the first work that I had done in over five years, and I was on a huge high. I felt invincible as I was aligned with my true life's purpose! What better way to celebrate than with champagne and a bit of a shake of my middle-aged booty with my one of my best friends!

Now, I am a big, tall, Germanic, pear-shaped woman, and men usually find me intimidating. They certainly never want to buy me drinks or engage in other acts of night-time chivalry that I see the petite, plastic girly girls get. So I was confused when guys were coming out of the woodwork to get my attention. I even had one guy trip me up so I would talk to him. Something was different. There must have been something glowing about me that night.

Later, as I was standing to the side having a breather from my dancing efforts (I'm a bit of a head-sweater so I have to pace

THE ACTUAL BEGINNING – A HAPPY TALE

myself if I don't want to look like a drowned rat!), I felt a looming presence next to me and a firm hand on my shoulder as a sultry voice whispered in my ear, 'This doesn't have to mean anything to you, but I just wanted to let you know that I think you are extraordinarily beautiful,' and then he gracefully walked away, leaving me floundering and gasping. I think I might have feebly said, 'Me too!' as he retreated, but thankfully he missed that!

Still in delicious shock that someone could say something so romantic to me, my friend Amanda shook me out of it and demanded to be told everything! As I filled her in, we headed over to the bar to recharge our glasses. Since he had made the first move, I knew that when I saw him again the next move would need to come from me. An equal exchange of energy. I casually surveyed the crowd for him and finally spotted him chatting with his friend on the other side of the bar. He was six foot, seven inches tall, complete with a stylish 1950s rockabilly vibe with a quiff and sideburns. So, so cool! I couldn't let this one get away.

As we slowly made our way towards where he and his friend were standing, we made eye contact. I knew from his look that I would find welcome company, so I walked over and said, 'After leaving me with a comment like that I feel I should at least know your name!' He looked down at me with a cheeky smile.

UNTANGLED

'But of course, Darling. It's Stuart and it's a delight to meet you.'

I don't recall any of our conversation after that in specific detail. But I do remember thinking he was one of the most absolutely charming men I'd ever met. It was as though he was a gentleman from another time when charm and chivalry ruled. He laughed with his whole body and a cheeky gleam in his eyes. There was a gentle kindness to him combined with such lightning fast, wicked humour. I was a goner!

It finally came time to either go home or find the next place for just one more drink. Not wanting to end the night, the four of us meandered down the road a bit further to the next late-night venue where we played pool, drank and made merry. We also added to the list of our friendships made that night a rather elderly, moustachioed, wild-haired, bohemian dude called Zoran. He was one of those generous, larger-than-life personalities that can come across to some as a bit too forceful and obnoxious. Luckily for Zoran, we were all loved up and welcomed him into the fold with open arms!

When last drinks were called, Zoran announced, in his flamboyant fashion, that he was the proud owner of a restaurant nearby and would love for us to go there so he could cook for us! What untold generosity was this? Would we get there to find it was an undercover human trafficking operation and we were

THE ACTUAL BEGINNING – A HAPPY TALE

his next victims? Feeling wild and reckless, we all decided to find out.

After shivering in the cold, waiting for Zoran to unlock the door and turn on the lights, we all stepped warily over the threshold and were delighted to be in a beautiful open space with tan leather banquettes lining one wall and a long, elegant bar along the other.

Zoran pushed bottles of wine into our arms as he ushered us into one of the banquettes then dashed off into the kitchen to prepare a series of platters of delicious food for us. His generosity astounded all of us – in fact, the whole night had been astonishing!

Stuart and I ate and drank, laughed and flirted outrageously. I kept thinking that I needed to find an opportunity to kiss him as being a bad kisser is such a deal-breaker for me and everything was going so perfectly. I finally found my chance when he went upstairs to the bathroom. I waited a few minutes then followed discreetly. When I got to the top of the stairs, he was waiting for me. He opened his arms and enfolded me in his warmth as we kissed.

We were together from that moment onwards.

Everyone who met him loved him. Stuart was an extraordinary man from another time. He was always debonair and

UNTANGLED

delightful. When he was with you, you felt like the only one in the room, as if he was sharing a naughty secret with only you. He laughed until his shoulders were sore from shaking. He wept with pride every time he saw me painting in my studio. He was wickedly funny. He called everyone 'Darling' but we all knew that he was really the darling one.

CHAPTER 3

Hospital

After the family meeting with the doctors, I guess we were all fairly devastated. I certainly didn't know what to think or how to be. To try and gain some sense of control in this new reality, I went into a default mode of disconnection, conditioned from years of customer service, and hid behind my mask of niceness, cut off from how I truly felt.

When I went in to see Stuart, he was sitting up in his hospital bed looking so vague and yellow. I felt so angry at him for doing this and so unbearably sad that this was happening. I didn't want to feel this way, I didn't want to see reality.

Once word got out that Stuart was in hospital and not likely to be coming out, everyone came out of the woodwork. He was so well loved. He became a public figure. It was no longer my relationship with him but a social frenzy with Stu holding court. He was always so polite, charming and funny with everyone. The end of visiting hours was the time when I could be alone with him, but he was just so spent, as was I. I couldn't reach him behind his social mask that had been in place all day, and I couldn't reach myself for exactly the same reasons. Exhausted after the social rounds, I would simply lie next to him on the hospital bed. Peaceful and calming.

Maybe I should have used those moments to talk about what was really going on and ask about what he wanted. Did he want to stay? Did he realise he was dying? But I didn't. I guess I was a bit of a coward. To be fair on myself, I knew that with his illness he was caught up in a mind fog. I knew instinctively that I couldn't reach him.

It's funny how things fall into a routine so quickly. I would wake each day to at least a minimum of 30 voice messages and texts from Stuart's friends checking in on how he was doing before I even walked into the hospital.

When I think of the routine at the hospital, I see it from a bird's-eye view, watching us chatting to Stu, or when things got too much or the room was too full, walking to the lounge area with its sterile grey walls and garish blue, patterned carpet,

HOSPITAL

walking into the attached kitchenette to make cups of tea, debrief or to just have a minute of space. That lounge held us all over those two weeks. So many of Stuart's friends would arrive pale and wild-eyed with shock as they had just heard the news for the first time. Stu's family and I became the message bearers and the counsellors, telling the story of how Stuart got there, that he was probably going to die but that we had hope, and holding people as they had their breakdowns. How I envied them their freedom to do that. I felt nothing at that stage. I was frozen. *Maybe I can wail later when this is done*, I thought.

It was at that point of burnout that I realised I needed help. I felt I was supporting everyone and that there was no one there for me. It was all about Stuart. Which is understandable, after all, he was the patient. But when your life gets hijacked and every waking moment, every thought and every feeling is about the patient, and you have no needs of your own or an identity anymore, it becomes unsustainable and unbearable.

In any hour of need, I have always called upon my mum, and this was definitely one of those times. We had always been close and I needed her love, warmth, cheeky humour and support around me, so I rang and asked her to come to Melbourne. She was in Queensland at the time as she was doing her grey nomad retirement caravan trip around Australia. She left my stepfather and the caravan somewhere near Brisbane and caught the next flight out to be with me. I also called upon the support of one of my dearest friends, Rick, to come over from Adelaide. He had been my manager at a restaurant that I'd worked in a decade before and had ended up becoming one of my best friends. He was someone who had seen it all so I knew I could always confide in him and he would never judge me.

My mum and Rick were so amazing, and I will forever be so grateful for their friendship and the support they offered me. They would take me out to lunch as I usually forgot to eat, and they would sit and chat to each other, allowing me the space to just be. They would even order for me as at that point I couldn't even decide what I wanted to eat or drink, I was just so exhausted and disconnected from my needs. No one demanded anything of me in that space. I felt loved and protected. A bit of light amid the shit. But eventually they both had to go home. Their kindness was the respite I needed to help me get through the next stage.

Stu would be up all night going to the bathroom as the drugs he was given were a diuretic. He had painful, enormous haemorrhoids that needed cream. The nursing staff where stretched, and Stuart was getting worse. Two of Stu's friends offered to stay the night and nurse him, which was incredible! Sometimes humans are amazing! We then decided that we would spread

HOSPITAL

the shifts between the three of us. I'm not sure how they coped as we never discussed personal issues, just how Stuart had been doing. But I knew that I was in a waking hell!

Just before visiting hours ended, I would drive home to shower and have something to eat. My wonderful flatmate, Janna, would have dinner for me and do my washing. What a legend! Then I would head back to the hospital and roll out a foam mattress on the hospital floor and get ready for the night's activity.

Stuart was exhausted after all the socialising, so he was usually out of it. I would feed him dinner as his hands had become too shaky. He would toss and turn all night. I would catch snippets of broken sleep in between until he would wake up, disorientated and needing to go to the bathroom. I would leap up and grab him and his IV drip and help them both navigate the way. After every trip I would have to put cream on the haemorrhoids. Sometimes we didn't make it to the bathroom in time. Everything about Stuart both inside and out was yellow, and there was a sweet, sickly smell emanating from his skin that I thought I would never get out of my nostrils. The sheer horror of seeing someone I loved be reduced to that pathetic, emaciated, yellow stranger will always stay with me.

Still believing he would get better (there was some

success from the drugs) and being horrified at the reconstituted cardboard masquerading as hospital food, I started to bring in fresh low-sodium meals. It sounds tasteless, but I swear it was yummy! Even with all the toxins floating around in his bloodstream as his liver and kidneys were fucked, he was still craving salty foods. The doctors told me that any salt would kill him. He wasn't even allowed painkillers because of the toxic overload. It was heartbreaking to have to say 'no' when he said he was in pain. Painkillers then became the new alcohol as Stuart would beg his friends for them. I'm sure there were a few snuck in. I was so terrified that if he had any that we would lose him, and I just needed to get him over the hurdle and strong again and everything would be ok.

In the end it didn't matter because the drugs didn't work. He ended up falling into a coma. I had unknowingly brought in his last meal – sushi and sashimi from our favourite Japanese restaurant. But no soy sauce as it is too high in sodium. I mean, why didn't I get it? I still thought he was going to make it. All he wanted to eat was deep-fried, salty chicken wings from a takeaway place he used to visit in happier times. That's all he wanted: some painkillers and salty, fried chicken wings, and I wouldn't let him because I didn't want to be the one that killed him. This fills me with such shame that I could have denied a

HOSPITAL

lovely human what he wanted, his choice of last meal. That I let my fear override everything.

I had never seen someone die before. I don't think you can ever be prepared. Just watching and waiting while they shut down. It freaked me out so much that I was sitting there watching him dehydrate and starve to death, and I couldn't do a thing to help. I remember thinking he looked like a baby budgerigar with its beak open, rounded tongue gasping for water.

I remember on the last night coming back home to shower and have something to eat and update everyone. When I left to go back to the hospital, around 10:30 pm, just as I was about to get into the car I felt this enormous sense of peace, that everything is going to be ok. When I looked at Stu that night, he looked peaceful after all the turmoil. The fight had gone. I looked closer and, even though his body was still there, Stuart's essence had gone.

I sat down beside the bed, a cup of tea in hand, with Stu's dad on the other side of him, to wait until the finish. For us to be the witnesses of Stuart's last breath. I was watching his steady breathing and all of a sudden he jerked forward as if wanting to tell us something important. He let out a deep sigh. It was his last.

After pronouncing him dead, the doctor left and we were

UNTANGLED

left alone with Stuart's body. A calm serenity filled the space as Stuart's dad and I sat in silence and drank cups of tea, all the while with Stu lying between us. Just before dawn broke, I looked down and saw all these beautiful splashes of colour in shades of peach and sky-blue shimmering all over Stuart's body. I'm so glad I had that last piece of beauty to hold on to and remember.

CHAPTER 4

The aftermath

The aftermath of someone dying is a strange, surreal beast. Once they have finished the fight between living and dying, there is a reassuring sense of peace and calm. There is nothing more you can do – they have gone. I found that there was a serene silence to life, as if it was having a minute of silence to honour another beautiful soul leaving the planet.

But this sense of peace and serenity eventually passed, and I was left with the feeling that a nuclear bomb had combusted within me and I was a walking, toxic wasteland.

I guess when you go through something so traumatic it feels as though you are the only one on the planet who feels the same way, and no one can understand or relate to you. I mean,

UNTANGLED

how on earth can you find the words to express the inexpressible? I couldn't even untangle all the complex emotions for my own understanding let alone try and tell someone else. I didn't understand what had just happened.

I wish I could look back on these memories and say that I allowed the grief to flow, that I allowed myself to feel everything, that I was gracious. But I didn't. I froze. I wasn't equipped to deal with any of it. I barely knew how to be an adult let alone deal with this wild emotional landscape – the emotions were just too intense. But really, who the hell is ready to deal with any of that anyway? No one can prepare you for that. It is just too experiential.

At one point when it became too much, I reached out and rang a grief counsellor and also read up on the seven stages of grief. At that point I might have learnt some resourceful ways for dealing, but I just felt more disconnected and withdrew. I couldn't relate to anything that was said about the grieving process. The way I was grieving didn't seem to fall neatly into any of the stages. I was in the middle of an out-of-control hot mess … hoping that I would wake up and it would all go away.

In actual fact, if I had really looked, I would have found that I was experiencing a classic case of denial and shock. I was in denial of denial! I was so far into denial that I couldn't even

THE AFTERMATH

remember what Stuart looked like. It felt like it had happened another lifetime ago to somebody else.

Life became a social whirlwind. Luckily for me, I had such a wonderful network of friends who came to support me. Almost every night for a month I had friends come over to visit, bearing food and booze. We ate, drank and laughed, really full hearty belly laughs. It was the most social time of my life! It was as though I had never been with Stuart at all and the incident in the hospital had never happened. I had picked up the threads of a life from an alternate reality. I even dyed my hair white-blonde to fit in with that new version of me in that new life. Stripping the colour of my hair meant that there would be no evidence of the person I was before.

I remember at Stuart's wake, a lady I'd never met before came up to me and gave me a slip of paper with her phone number. Her husband had died nine months previously and she asked me to call her if I ever needed support. 'Because in three months' time, everyone goes back to their own lives, and you are left alone.' And it was completely true! Everyone, now that they had been reassured that I was coping well (little did they know!), did go back to their own lives and moved on.

There was the voice inside my head insidiously whispering, sometimes shouting that I had to move on and get on with my life. Just get over it! I mean, I REALLY wanted to! I didn't want to be in that frozen limbo. I had absolutely no idea how to do that though. It became an apathetic acceptance of this low-frequency pain that I couldn't quite pinpoint or feel directly. Just a constant white noise.

I noticed people would be weird around me. Sometimes people didn't even know that Stuart had died and would freak out when I told them. When I say 'freak out' what I mean is that there is some weird social protocol that we must absorb when growing up that leaves us ill-equipped to deal with real, meaty, intense shit, and people freeze and say disconnecting things like 'My condolences' or 'Sorry for your loss'. I mean, really! What the fuck are condolences anyway, and have you ever used them in any other sentence structure before? No! It's just a rote saying you use when faced with someone's pain. Even people I knew well would say this to me. Trust me, it doesn't make anyone feel better. I just felt even more distant and strange when those empty words were uttered. I would have much preferred an 'Oh my god, that is so absolutely shit!' Something equally raw that speaks to the devastating reality of the situation.

One of the things I found hard about grieving, or attempting to grieve, is that people are uncomfortable with seeing someone cry. If I started to tear up in conversation, they would try and fix it

THE AFTERMATH

by hugging me and telling me that it's all going to be alright. In fact, I would find myself comforting them because they would get so distressed. I would squash everything down again and tell them that I was ok. That social conditioning choked my grief and stunted its expression when what I needed was the opposite. I just needed someone to allow the intensity, to not fix anything but just give me the space to cry, to let it come up and out of me so I could release a fraction of the giant iceberg within me.

CHAPTER 5

Back to hospitality

Everyone went back to their lives, and I felt left behind in the looming shadow of the unknown. I had no idea what my next steps were supposed to be, so I took a deep breath and I went with the most obvious. My rent was months behind, and bills were stacking up. It was time to get a job!

I had left my event styling job when Stuart was in hospital as I couldn't handle any more stress and drama in my life than was already there. Maybe I could go back to my hospitality days and get some waitressing work?

This was when I bumped into a chef I'd worked with eight years prior at a beautiful French bistro in Melbourne's CBD.

Chef Scotty was always an abrasive, cocky, arrogant son of

a bitch, and I liked him. He was always so passionate about food and incredibly ambitious, which clearly carried him through the hard yards of Melbourne's kitchens to start his own chain of restaurants. I'm so proud of his drive and vision. (Still arrogant as fuck though!)

Chef Scotty got me a job where he was working at a local gastro pub in North Melbourne. A stunning building with beautiful Art Nouveau stained-glass windows and a lovely, low-key local vibe. It was owned by another chef we had both worked with, so I just walked right on in and started.

I will always be forever grateful for Chef Scotty's brusque kindness and generosity to me in those days. It saved me for a time. Gave me some normalcy, stability and focus. Almost like nothing had happened, making a fresh start. Almost. The funny thing about grief, though, is that it can strike out of nowhere.

It was towards the end of my shift; the kitchen had closed, and I was moving guests into the front bar to finish off their drinks. As I was pouring champagne for a lovely couple, the guy popped an engagement ring in her champagne when she wasn't looking. I'm always a bit dubious about this kind of behaviour, like putting the ring in the dessert, for instance. What are the odds that they don't see it and swallow it whole? Do they wait till it does its thing through the digestive system and then propose? Or wait until she stops choking and give her a good whack on the back to dislodge it and then propose? Neither of these things happened; she was delighted, said yes, necked the champagne and he popped the ring on her finger. It was a very joyous occasion with the good will of everyone at the bar. The couple was ecstatic. I was truly happy for them and oohed and aahed when the ring was thrust in my face.

But then out of nowhere the hand of grief came and smacked me in my face! I could feel the pressure of violent emotion building up in my chest and ran out of the bar into the broom cupboard under the stairs and broke down. In the safety of darkness and an enclosed space amongst the vacuum, brooms and cleaning products, I cried and wailed for hours as the waves hit me. I finally staggered out, puffy-eyed and tear-stained. No one said anything. I don't think anyone noticed, which I am forever grateful for. To be so out of control in a public space was embarrassing to me. But no one checked the broom cupboard, so it went under the radar.

There were other occasional breakdowns. Sometimes on trams and in other random places when I smelled a familiar scent or heard a song that reminded me of him, and with Stu being a musician, there were many! But I began to recognise a familiar pressure in my chest and throat and became an expert at cutting it off and shoving it back down.

Life passed by in hospitality in a bit of a drunken whirl. Jobs changed, there were new faces, new menus and wine lists, more knock-off beverages and more boozy late nights.

I had mixed feelings about drinking … After such an experience, why on earth would I continue?, I wondered. The only way I can reconcile it is that booze seemed to be the only source of self-soothing that I could access at the time. I just wanted to feel a bit of joy. Booze allowed me to feel carefree and silly. Life was more spontaneous, fun and adventurous. I wanted to be as far away from my internal iceberg as I could, no matter the cost.

Hospitality was a perfect place to hide from grief. In fact, the actual job of working in customer service is to squash your needs down and run around looking after other people. No time to think about what you want or how you feel. Then, when service is all done and the customers have gone home, it's our time to claim the holy grail of the shift … our knock-off drink! Front of house and back of house all come together to share a staff meal and many beverages while telling our war stories from the evening, like a dysfunctional, loving family should. After bonding over our shared experiences, the more hardened of us continued on while the others that had family and loved ones went home.

UNTANGLED

I guess that it was the need to belong, to be part of that weird family, that kept me there. They held the key to another life where I could be happy and free for just a moment. I could interrupt my grief and be someone else. A fun, free, larger-than-life person.

CHAPTER 6

Nine months later

I found it to be such a weird, disconnected stage as I was part of a new life yet emotionally still exactly where I had been nine months before: still grieving, not ok at all but still feeling as though I had to participate in life. After all, everyone else had moved on.

I felt the heaviness and the burden of being associated with someone who had died. I felt like it tainted all my relationships by everyone pitying me for being Stuart's widow. I felt that no one saw me clearly anymore.

I stopped seeing Stu's family because it was too heartbreaking. A constant reminder of our collective sadness weighing us all down.

UNTANGLED

Even though the last thing I wanted was people's pity, I discovered the manipulative power that pity could wield if I chose to use it. I found that in certain situations if I wanted to get out of doing something or if I wanted someone to do something for me, I only had to tell people that my partner had died. People would freak out and then bend over backwards to make it ok for me.

    I was hyper-aware of this but I didn't want to be a victim of grief. To always be identified with the loss of my partner. I wanted to be more than that. I wanted to be free. Free from everything associated with this shitty story that I felt trapped in!

    Around that time some life insurance money came through. Not a massive amount but enough to pay for the things that felt important to me. Once the backlog of debts from Stuart's days had been paid and rent payments were under control, I decided that going overseas might be my way out of all of this mess. I wanted out of my life! I felt I had outgrown Melbourne and needed to find a new life overseas. Maybe in Tokyo or Berlin or New York? I was going to reinvent myself and get a fresh start!

    I wanted to be a world traveller, be free and embrace all experiences. I thought I would find myself again and find the city and the people that were right for me. But instead, I caused myself so much needless pain and wasted so much money.

NINE MONTHS LATER

I look back at this time and wish I could have been kinder to myself. Instead of buying that plane ticket, I wish I could have stayed still a bit longer and tuned into what would be the most loving, nurturing options for me. Maybe go to a healing retreat for a couple of months? I wish I had, but the need to escape was too strong.

CHAPTER 7

Japan

As I think back to that time, most details are hazy and yet some are crystal clear. I can remember the dramatic emotional moments and the details of where I was at the time, but the gentler, everyday moments have faded.

Back then there were no smartphones, and the internet wasn't the dependable, wise friend that it is now, information at your fingertips. I had to depend on the numerous Lonely Planet books that I had bought for all the countries that I planned to visit. My suitcase weighed a tonne!

I remember seeing the movie *Lost in Translation* a few years before my trip, and I saw myself as Scarlett Johansson's character, a wandering tourist losing themselves in the culture and

JAPAN

vibrancy of Tokyo. I wanted that escape. I wanted to connect with the place, see amazing sights – I wanted to forget my story.

My lovely friend Pat had been living and teaching English in Tokyo for a couple of years and had a little apartment that I could go stay in. Unfortunately for me, Pat was leaving to visit Borneo on the day that I was arriving, so we were like ships in the night with a tiny crossover period for a quick cup of tea and a whirlwind tour of her apartment and the local area.

I'm so glad I had the tour or else there was no way that I would have been able to operate the bathroom or the toilet! Apparently, a standard in Japanese apartments and I had heard stories but had never seen or experienced anything quite like it! The temperature of the air, the water and floor in the bathroom could be programmed to your perfect desired requirements. The same with the toilet, but with the addition of a heated toilet seat. This was a bit too creepy for me as it felt as someone had just been there!

Around the corner from the apartment was the local konbini, a 7-Eleven convenience store on steroids! There was rockmelon with delicate patterns on its skin presented in gold leaf wrapping. There was beef tartare with intricate marbling to take away. Rice bento boxes with eggs, tofu, chicken and beef cutlets and more. I had never seen anything like it. In Australia, then the most you'd expect at the end of the day would be a hardened, dry sausage roll that's been sitting in the pie warmer for too long!

My first day was not noteworthy. I was mainly navigating the train system and saw a temple or two and then got lost for a while. I managed to get on the right train with the help of two lovely train station hostesses who had some English and find my way back to the apartment.

The next day, after consulting my Lonely Planet guidebook, I decided that I would see the Great Buddha (Daibutsu) down the coast near Kamakura. I got on the JR Yokosuka Line and got off at Kita-Kamakura Station. The plan was to visit the nearby Jochiji Temple then saunter along the Daibutsu walking trail among some Japanese woodland until I came across the Daibutsu itself, then pop into the Hase-dera temple and see the goddess of compassion before walking a bit further to get on the train at Hase Station to return to Tokyo.

I remember hopping out on the platform at Kita-Kamakura and wondering where the hell I was. I thought it would be a large, well-signed major station. But no, it was a quaint little country dinky-doo stop with not that much signage and no one around!

I clutched my Lonely Planet with sweaty fingers while faith-

JAPAN

fully following a tiny map. When I came upon the stone steps of the Jochiji Temple, I breathed in a calming cleansing breath, and took in the graceful line of weathered stone leading up to the main temple gate. It was straight out of a postcard, untouched by Westerners. I could almost see the Buddhist monks making their way gracefully and tranquilly up to the temple.

The main building, Donge Doh, which is named after a legendary flower that opens only once every 3,000 years, houses the Buddhist trinity statues representing past, present and future. Apparently, they are meant to listen to our every wish, and wish I did.

After I had wished myself out, I meandered through the beautiful, tranquil gardens and came across a lovely shrine dug into the cliff. This beautiful buddha with a big belly was tucked inside with offerings of flowers at his feet. I stood at a respectful distance and said a little prayer, or at least that is what I thought was the right thing to do at the time.

As I had my head bent mid-prayer, a young Japanese family barrelled past me and started laughing and rubbing his belly. Apparently, this was Hotei-son, one of the seven gods of Kamakura, and rubbing his belly will make you happy. That's what the laughing Japanese family told me with their big smiles and belly-rubbing gestures! So, once they had moved on, I went up and did a thorough rub of his belly, and his bald head for good measure! I'm not sure if this made me happy but the laughter and joy of the Japanese family certainly did. Just a little bit of lightness. Maybe the three buddhas had heard my wish and Hotei-son granted it!

With a lighter heart I found my way to the start of the Daibutsu walking trail, or at least that is what I thought it was. Since I have been doing some research, retracing my steps, I have found that it is not a gentle, short walking path but actually called a hiking course that takes an hour to 90 minutes and taking water, snacks and good walking shoes is strongly recommended!

Now, let me tell you that I am without doubt NOT a hiker or a sporty person of any kind and for some reason I ALWAYS seem to have on inappropriate footwear for the occasion! Like the time I decided to go on a little tour of Ireland when I was in my late 20s. I had never been on one before and certainly wasn't equipped, unlike the two New Zealanders on the same tour. They were fully equipped with their hiking boots, windbreakers, weatherproof outfits and backpacks. I, on the other hand, was wearing black tights and skirt, a red skivvy with a very nice tan corduroy jacket, a red umbrella for wet weather, an over-the-shoulder handbag and black Cuban-heeled boots. I climbed up and down every Irish cliff front that they all did and I did it in style!

Now that I think about it, I was in a very similar outfit for this hike. Maybe I do have a signature style after all! So then, with my signature outfit, inappropriate footwear, no water, no snacks, certainly no Google Maps and no idea, I headed off into the Kamakura Western Hills Woodlands.

The woodlands were so lush and leafy with a dirt path to follow, quite picturesque. Such promise, quite living up to my expectations; I mean, how hard could the walk be? I guess it's not that hard if you're prepared, but I wasn't as I climbed over tree roots and steep steps, up and down hills until I felt totally and utterly lost. There just didn't seem to be any signage or any reference for me, just never-ending forest and the dirt path.

Panic built as I came to a fork in the path with only more of the same dense forest in both directions. I sat down on the path and cried. I had a moment of absolute abandonment. Here I was on my own, lost in a Japanese forest, no one knew that I was here, no one was expecting me, and no one would be missing me. How did I get to this point in my life, my existence meaning nothing?

After the panic and sadness passed and the soothing whispering of the trees had calmed me, I stood up and started following my intuition. I continued on the never-ending pathway and finally came to a break in the trees where I could see houses and the coastline in the distance. Still with no idea of where I was, I felt comforted by signs of civilisation. It encouraged me to keep going along the path where eventually I came across the entrance to the Daibutsu.

 The Great Buddha, when I came upon it, was majestic. A beautiful bronze statue sitting serenely at almost 12 metres high. I was in awe at the sheer size and expansiveness of the buddha. I had never seen anything quite like it before in my life. Apparently, it was cast in 1252 and was housed in a large temple hall but over the 14th and 15th centuries, with typhoons and tsunamis, the temple buildings were destroyed multiple times and the Great Buddha had been in the open air since the late 15th century.

 When I think about it, what I find most beautiful is that there was this stunning creation that had been sitting and enduring wild weather beating at its structure for over 500 years and still it was there, still it endures and thrives, giving pleasure to all that look upon it.

 I got a glimmer of hope. Maybe if I can get through this, to endure this grief path, the path that feels exactly like the Daibutsu trail experience, then maybe I will find the beauty in all

JAPAN

this? Maybe I might even eventually thrive?

With hope, onwards I went to the next Buddhist temple, the Hase-dera. That temple houses the 11-headed statue of Kannon, the goddess of mercy and compassion. She is a regal, gilded, over nine-metre-tall wooden statue. Legend has it that two Kannon statues were carved out of one sacred tree. One was enshrined in the Hase-dera temple in Nara (Japan's original capital, outside Kyoto) and the other one was thrown into the ocean after praying for it to be washed up somewhere else to save others through her mercy. Which she did some 15 years later and the Hase-dera temple was built to enshrine her.

Walking a bit further through the beautiful gardens of the Hase-dera temple and down the stone steps, I came across Jizo-do Hall. This stood out to me as extraordinarily bittersweet and touching. Thousands of stone Jizo statues all lined up, representing all the unborn children lost to miscarriages, abortions or stillbirths. They are known as Mizuko, meaning Water Children, as they have never breathed the air. They have only known the water of the womb. Some of them had brightly coloured knitted beanies and shawls. The fact that someone had taken the time to dress their lost child's statue, to tend to them, to honour them, to pay tribute to their spirit, moved me deeply.

UNTANGLED

I saw the ritual and honour in everyday Japanese culture. Everywhere you turn there is a beautiful temple giving an opportunity to unburden yourself and allow yourself to surrender to the possibility that maybe everything is taken care of by some kind of divine intervention and that maybe you can just relax and get on with your life.

There was nothing in my own culture or experience like it that I felt I could turn to. The closest that I could think of would be walking into a church, but its history is so laden with heaviness and darkness, and I certainly didn't need any more of that!

It was late by the time I got back to Tokyo as I think I had taken another wrong turn and instead of a short five-minute walk to Hase Station, I walked what felt like an eternity to Kamakura Station. I popped into my local konbini and got myself some delicious takeaway sushi and sake and headed back to the apartment to make my plans for the next day.

The plan was to go to the Shibuya district and take in the neon frenzy, cross a couple of times over the famous pedestrian crossing, and then go to Yoyogi Park to spot a Harajuku girl in their zany cosplay outfits. I loved the whole contrast of regal, serene, spiritual Japan one day and then my *Lost in Translation* city adventure the next. But that day didn't happen because my personal tsunami arrived before breakfast time.

JAPAN

Being on my own in Tokyo was the first time that I had truly stopped distracting myself since Stuart had died. I had no friends to call, no job to lose myself in, it was just me. I was the one responsible for my survival in a foreign land with no support. Why I had set that up for myself is beyond me. While my guard was down, all the emotions that had been biding their time, lurking beneath my social veneer, now violently erupted!

My tears, once escaped, were uncontrollable. My emotions were so intense and overwhelming that I couldn't isolate and define them. They just smashed against me relentlessly and the only way that I knew how to cope with them was just to cry. I stayed in that apartment and cried for three days straight. I made my world small so I could feel an element of being in control of it, but I wasn't in control of anything. I would have panic attacks just going to the local konbini for food. Eventually I even stopped doing that. If it wasn't for the fact that I had a pre-booked ticket on the bullet train to Kyoto, then I might very well still be there!

Eventually, I did nervously emerge from that apartment and made my way to Kyoto. I went straight to my hotel where I met up with my friend Rick who had just flown in from Australia that morning. I didn't tell him about my Tokyo apartment tsunami. I wanted to pretend that it never happened and that it was out of my system. He saved me, yet again, exactly as he had done when Stuart was in hospital, giving me respite from myself, giving me distraction from my story. What a relief that I could laugh and receive the support that our beautiful friendship offered.

Rick has always reminded me of Cary Grant. A lover of good food, wine, culture, a true world traveller with boundless compassion for everyone and a true confidante. I always feel totally accepted for myself, and life is always more fun in his presence.

We had timed our trip for the sakura (cherry blossom) season, and it was worth it. Canals lined with candy pink cherry blossoms, and temples and shrines abounded! Kyoto was a magical mix of history and the modern with stunning geisha twirling their parasols, gracefully gliding over the curved wooden bridges past brightly lit game arcades and neon billboards.

We had a full day of walking under the cherry blossoms from temple to temple. The soft pinks and white of the sakura petals contrasting with the soft, moss-covered grounds of the temples. Truly a visual feast! Sakura is a time of hope and renewal as it heralds the spring but also because of its short blooming time – cherry blossoms symbolise the transience of life. How appropriate! But for my internal world there was no

JAPAN

sakura season in sight. I was still in the middle of my winter, but at least, for that moment anyway, I had the warmth of friendship.

At night we would explore Kyoto's vibrant restaurant and bar scene. On one of those nights, we found an amazing, hip restaurant. It was so cool that they wouldn't let us in! Because we were Westerners they thought we wanted the easy tourist experience and told us to move on to one of the many other eating houses with the plastic food displayed in their front windows. We spent 10 minutes pleading at the door to give us a chance, that we were from hospitality too and we were so up for a food and wine experience!

Thankfully they relented and we walked through the clean, ultra-modern interior and were seated in a cosy banquette with bamboo dividers. Our waiter, a super-chill Kyoto local, studying art and sporting a funky peroxide blonde hairdo, looked after us beautifully. We tried everything he suggested and everything that was a speciality of the house. We ordered delicious wines and poured glasses for our waiter and chef to try. Once the customers had all left, the chef, our waiter and all the rest of the staff joining our table had a lock in. A lock in is where a restaurant or bar closes, the doors are locked and you continue drinking and being merry with the staff. I highly recommend it, and it is made all the sweeter when it is totally unexpected!

UNTANGLED

On another night we found this lovely, little local 10-seater restaurant and perched ourselves up at the bar to watch the action of the chefs. We were having a lovely time, sharing dishes, eating off very pretty, ornate blue and gold ceramic plates, when we noticed everyone laughing and pointing at us. I had no idea why as we weren't doing anything out of the usual. Maybe because we were the only non-Japanese people there? It was getting a bit ridiculous, so I asked the bar staff what was so funny? Apparently the blue and gold ceramic plates that we had been eating off weren't actually dinner plates. They were ashtrays! Dinner didn't taste so good after that!

On our final day we caught the train to Nara and visited the Todai-ji temple that houses the Daibutsu. It is the largest in the world, and the scale of this buddha was immense. The context of the hall housing the buddha just added to the grandeur. I stood at its feet in awe of its beauty and serenity. But to be completely honest, even though it looked like the shit sibling in comparison, I still preferred the Kamakura Daibutsu. Its strength and tenacity in enduring the elements made it more beautiful, in my eyes, than the pampered Nara Daibutsu, safe and dry in its gilded temple. I guess I was overlaying my experience so far on these beautiful statues. They were my metaphor for my life at that point. I desperately wanted to be safe, secure, pampered

JAPAN

and looked after but life had thrown me out into the elements, and I felt battered and out of control. But, unlike the Kamakura Daibutsu, I was yet to find my inner beauty and serenity.

Rick's friendship had made Kyoto a safe haven for me after Tokyo's tsunami and I didn't want to leave its sakura-laden streets. Unfortunately for me, like the sakura, the season of safety was over after a short burst of beauty. Rick left and made his way to Osaka to explore a bit more of Japan while I navigated my way back to Tokyo and made my way to the next unknown – Berlin.

CHAPTER 8

Berlin Part 1

I feel something special about being up in an airplane. It doesn't matter if I have just left a shitstorm and am about to land in another, that time in the air is neutral. You don't have to do anything, be anything or go anywhere, because you can't! You just have to enjoy the ride and be taken care of. You are safe for that moment.

    The flight from Tokyo to Berlin gave me the reset I needed and I felt a sense of excitement as I exited the Berlin Airport. I felt the excitement of discovering a new city, a new adventure, and yet Berlin felt oddly familiar to me.

    I was staying in a new arty, funky hotel in the middle of the bustling artist scene in Mitte. The whole area had an exciting feel

BERLIN PART 1

of potential. Artists using empty spaces as theatres or pop-up galleries, uber cool bars and restaurants everywhere. It was like the artists were breathing beauty and life back to the old ruins of an area that had been given nothing for so long.

On my first day in Berlin, I embraced my inner nerd and went on a double-decker bus tour. It was so bittersweet seeing the stunning architecture of the city pockmarked with bullet holes and big gaps where buildings used to be. The gaps left from the bombings of the Second World War, destroyed buildings that never grew back. My breath was taken away at a vision of what this city would have looked like before the war. It must have been magnificent, like I imagine an ancient Roman empire to be with its beautiful white marble columns and stunning classical lines.

The recorded bus tour guide spoke of the Trümmerfrauen (rubble women) who, because of the shortage of men, barehanded, brick by brick moved around 75 million cubic metres of rubble from Berlin's streets left from the devastation of the bombings of WW2.

At the end of the war, the Allied forces in Germany ordered all women 15 to 50 years old to do the postwar clean up. They were responsible for tearing down the ruins of devastated buildings with basic tools like picks and sledgehammers, then breaking the rubble down to single bricks that would then be passed down long lines of bare-handed women to be cleaned and stacked for reconstruction.

How gruelling and overwhelming it must have been to be faced with that monumental task day in, day out. Such tenacity of the human spirit. I felt like I could do with a line of Trümmerfrauen to clear my internal rubble! Maybe that's why I resonated with their story, this shared sense of overwhelm in facing devastation and knowing there was no quick fix, only a step-by-step, brick-by-brick, 'follow the breadcrumbs' way of dealing with it.

But I wanted a quick fix! I couldn't bear sitting with this grief even though it was squashed as far down as it could go within me. I knew it was there, this low-level, dull pain. It was cutting me off from feeling any joy or happiness, and even being on the other side of the world as far away from my experience as I could get, I was still a prisoner of my grief. Still frozen.

I desperately wanted to be a world traveller meeting amazing people and having amazing, serendipitous moments of connection. I wanted to feel free and lighthearted. But being in a foreign country, not speaking the language and not knowing anyone, I contracted into myself. Grief keeps you small. Because it is overwhelming, because you can't control it, the mind flips out and thinks it can. I started creating routines for

BERLIN PART 1

myself to help self-soothe, to feel in control.

Every morning I would go to the same cafe near my hotel and order the same roll and order a coffee as these were the only things I knew how to ask for in German. The lovely guy who worked there, Ralph, spoke a little bit of English, so it helped. I would sit there for a couple of hours and just write in my journal. I definitely wasn't writing anything profound, just meaningless nonsense, but it gave me a sense of purpose.

When it started getting a bit weird with me being the only customer in that cafe for hours, and there is only so much coffee a girl can physically handle, I would reluctantly leave my safe haven, grab my clunky brick-like iPod and headphones and go wandering the streets, following the Torstraße, wandering through Alexanderplatz until I ended up on the grass of the Lustgarten park, looking at the Berliner Dom, the majestic Berlin Cathedral.

On my left, the Altes Museum, and to my right, the skeletal remains of the Palast der Republik. The government was having it demolished due to it being filled with asbestos. It was a hideous eyesore in contrast to the stunning Neo-Renaissance building of the Berliner Dom and the Neo-Classical Altes Museum.

I found out that back in 1950, the East German Government demolished the Berliner Schloss, a majestic baroque palace, and built the minimalist Palast der Republik on that site. Now here it was in tatters, being demolished only to have the Berliner Schloss rebuilt. Talk about the continuous cycle of creation, destruction and rebirth!

Berlin seemed to be showing me this cycle again and again, but I wasn't listening. I was trapped in the destruction stage and all I wanted was relief and sanctuary. So the Lustgarten park became another sanctuary for me. A place for me to feel as though I had somewhere to go, to give me purpose in my day.

I would sit there and long to go into the Altes Museum to see Queen Nefertiti's bust and other amazing Egyptian relics, to go inside the Berliner Dom and sit under its dome, see the Hohenzollern family crypt. But each time I'd walk to the entrance I would freeze. I couldn't go in! The idea of having to ask for a ticket for entry in German sent me into a wild frenzy of stress and panic. I was terrified, I was exhausted.

My days went on like this, a continuous loop, creating my own groundhog day. At night I would go to the same little Italian restaurant near my hotel, order the same pasta (spaghetti aglio e olio) and a glass or two, or maybe a bottle, of wine. There was a lovely waitress there, Hedda, who was also a travel agent and wanted to practise her English on me. It was a welcome reprieve to have someone to talk to, even if it was out of pity for my lonely state.

Then came another tsunami!

Like my Tokyo tsunami, I couldn't stop the ocean of tears. Hour after hour of crying left my eyes swollen to the point that I didn't recognise myself anymore. I couldn't leave the hotel. I stayed in there for days.

Crying gave no relief. It was relentless. When I thought about the past and what had happened, I cried. When I thought about my present I cried, and when I tried to think of my future I cried. Each state felt unbearable and hopeless. I didn't want to exist in any of them.

One evening I needed to get some fresh air so, in the cover of darkness with my deformed face, I went for a walk. Eyes to the ground, not daring to look up and make any human contact, I started on my well-worn pathway that I had already carved into the Berlin streets. I could hear the chatter and laughter of people walking past. The smells from the cafes and restaurants beckoned me to come inside and join them. But I was so overwhelmed with despair that I continued on.

Detouring off my pathway, I took a shortcut across the busy Torstraße. I stopped in the middle on a traffic island, waiting for the traffic to pass so I could cross to the other side. The fumes and the noise of the cars swept over me as I stood there. I felt so isolated. Then an insidious thought entered my mind: *Why don't I just end my life right here, right now?* I was exhausted and there seemed no point or hope for my existence. I saw an oncoming truck and I stepped out in front of it.

It reminded me of the time when I was 14 years old. I was one of those clumsy teenagers who was really uncomfortable in their bodies and in themselves. I had left everything I had known and had landed in a cold, unfriendly new town as Mum had moved us interstate. I had started in the middle of the year at an all-girls Catholic school. Everyone had known each other since primary school or earlier, so someone new was to be treated with the upmost suspicion and disdain. They were truly a tough crowd! Actually, they were a bunch of bitches!

I remember one time when my mum bought me some school shoes but had gotten them in men's sizing instead of women's by accident and I still had to go to school wearing them as we didn't have the money to purchase a second pair until Mum's next payday. I took them off for drama class and one of the girls picked them up and shouted, 'Who is wearing their dad's shoes to school?' They all laughed hysterically and when they realised they were mine they ran away with them and tried to flush them down the toilet. Needless to say, I didn't

BERLIN PART 1

have any friends. No one was interested in getting to know me. I would hide in the library at lunchtime. I was incredibly lonely and depressed.

I remember Mum would take us on picnics or go and do stuff as a family sometimes. Once, we were out on a bush walk and I had gone ahead on my own. I was walking along the top of a ravine and decided that I would climb down the cliff to get to the bottom before Mum and my sister. As I started climbing down, I stopped and looked down. I remember thinking how easy it would be to let go and just drop. To let go of my depressing, friendless life. It was a fleeting thought but it was the intensity of it that made it feel longer.

I had that same type of moment of intensity in Berlin. I felt I was walking out in front of the truck in slow motion, but the reality was just a split second of my foot landing on the street before I pulled it back again and the truck drove on past.

CHAPTER 9

Berlin Part 2

There is some part of me that no matter what happens insists that I choose life. I remember sitting in hospital looking at Stuart and knowing that he was choosing death and that I needed to let go and accept that. I remember at that thought, a rush of passion and certainty coursing through my system, knowing without a doubt that I choose life. It was not my time to go at 14 years old, hanging off a cliff, and neither was it my time in Berlin, no matter how hopeless and futile my life seemed at the time.

But I had scared myself and I needed help. I needed the support of my family and friends. I needed to be with people who loved me, and I needed to be in familiar safe territory. I

BERLIN PART 2

needed the resources to rebuild myself and heal. Maybe it was time to go home.

I felt too ashamed to go back and face my friends. Before I'd left, I had told them that I had outgrown Melbourne, that I was going to find a new city to live in, that I was going to embrace this new adventure and find a bigger, better, happier version of me. I couldn't go back so soon as this emotional wreck. I felt like such a failure and that was stronger than the need for support. So, I decided to stay and see the remainder of my trip through, four more days in Berlin and one week in New York. It seemed interminable!

The next morning, I went to my safe haven cafe and settled in to write in my journal (I had a lot to write about!). As Ralph came over with my coffee, we started chatting in our broken German and English. He asked if I wanted to join him and his friend later on for a drink. I was so surprised by his unexpected invitation that I nearly missed my mouth with my first sip of coffee. It sounded fun. After all, what did I really have to lose? So, I decided to go.

I met him and his friend Sara out the front of a quaint little pub with flowerpots everywhere, overflowing with brightly coloured pansies. The sun was shining. It was a beautiful spring day. We talked about life, travel and different cultures, and drank beer. It was such a delightful and unexpected experience. Such a welcome, loving interruption to my reality so far. As we parted ways, I left knowing that I had met some cool and kind-hearted humans.

That night at my safe haven dinnertime Italian restaurant, instead of my usual, I decided to have the linguine marinara. It was delicious. Hedda was on that night, and we got chatting. She asked me if I wanted to go out with her and her friend Elsa the next night!

What was happening? It seemed to me that once I had gotten as low as I could go and once I had decided that I wanted to stay, life came to meet me. I had been so caught up in my pain for so long that I had forgotten how to reconnect with the flow of life. I was a bit rusty, mistrusting and awkward but I decided that I would go along for the ride, and the next night that is exactly what I did!

The next evening, I met Hedda and Elsa in a cool, funky bar. It was so busy with such a dynamic energy. It reminded me of the Melbourne bar scene. I felt at home.

Elsa was the epitome of German beauty. She was tall, with long, blonde hair, high Germanic cheekbones and ice-blue eyes. She was gorgeous, vibrant and, although I didn't know it at the time, a loose caboose! After a few drinks there Elsa declared

BERLIN PART 2

it was boring and we should move onto the Kit Kat Club.

I had heard of the Kit Kat Club from the film and theatre show Cabaret so I was excited that we would be going to a classy cabaret bar, sitting down at little tables, drinking champagne and seeing a show. Awesome! Great call, Elsa.

We got into a taxi with Elsa in the front passenger seat, Hedda and me in the back. Our taxi driver, with his swarthy good looks and abundant black wavy hair, looked like a pirate and drove like an absolute madman!

At some point, once the g-force allowed, I opened my eyes to see Elsa groping our pirate taxi driver's crotch as he then leaned over and tried to stick his tongue as far down her throat as he could. I've got to admire his skills as he never once swerved and at no point did he slow down except to stop at an ATM for Elsa to take money out. I'm not sure if she did because the pirate taxi driver also got out and they were both gone for a solid 15 minutes while Hedda and I waited awkwardly in the backseat making small talk in our broken German and English. But some transaction definitely took place as when they returned, Elsa announced that our taxi ride was free!

The Kit Kat Club seemed to be in the middle of nowhere in some industrial estate. We walked up to what looked like an abandoned warehouse and went up a dingy stairwell into a blast of coloured neon light and scantily leather-clad bouncers waiting for us at the top. Apparently, I was overdressed for entry, so Hedda and Elsa started stripping off my layers until I was left in my black bra and knickers. That was definitely not what I had expected to happen, and it was not the classy little cabaret club that I had imagined with little round tables and lamps around the stage with flowing bottles of champagne. No, this appeared to be a fetish sex club with every walk of life there in latex, leather and all things kinky!

Trance music was pumping and sweaty dancers were glowing in the dim blue neon. I lost sight of Elsa and Hedda, but I didn't care because I felt strangely safe. I felt welcomed and accepted by my new friends on the dancefloor. Gimps, dominatrices, amputees were my new friends. We danced, we bought each other drinks, we laughed. It felt so freeing to be in such a radically different world that was not hostile and accepted me as I was. As I stood there in the middle of the Kit Kat Club in my bra and knickers, I thought, as I did when lost in the Japanese forest, that no one knows where I am, and they might not believe me even if they did! And for the first time since leaving Australia I felt that it was all going to be ok.

After my big night out (although a bit hung over), I felt a bit more confident to branch out of my self-imposed routine. So, I

BERLIN PART 2

decided I would try a new restaurant that the hotel I was staying in had recommended. As I came up to its stylish glass frontage, I could see the place was packed. It had a rustic, minimal French bistro vibe with an open kitchen on the left and a big blackboard menu. It felt intimidating, but I made myself walk in and ask for a table in my bad, halting German. The cool hipster waiter took pity on me and sat me up at the bench overlooking the kitchen, which was perfect for me. It gave me something to do. I felt part of the action as I swivelled in my seat, narrowly missing waiters grabbing the meals the chefs were plating up in front of me. I felt like I was back in the heart of my hospitality family.

They all looked after me so well, took the time to talk with me, the chefs would send me little tastes of food and the waiters kept my wine topped up. After feeling so shit about myself for so long, that was a balm to my soul! Hospitality therapy!

I ordered a beautiful bottle of wine and bought one for the staff to try as well. This simple gesture ensured my entry into my German hospitality family and, for the second time on my overseas trip, once everyone had left, I had another lock in with the staff! Lots of wine and laughter flowed and even more food came out. Then came the call for another venue and one more drink!

We all piled into a taxi (no frisky pirate taxi driver this time!)

and headed off to a local nightclub. After the previous night's shenanigans, the nightclub was tame and mainstream but still super cool and stylish.

Throughout the night, one of the chefs, Denz, had been making eyes at me. It was the first time anyone had looked that way at me in a very long time and the thought of being seen was both thrilling and terrifying. After quite a few drinks, and within the safety of low lighting, we both felt emboldened to lean over and have a kiss. It was delightful and warming, a little oasis in the heart of Berlin.

I was leaning with my arm over the back of the couch trying to appear cool when Denz asked me to go out to dinner with him the next day as it was his day off. What a wonderful invitation, to be asked out to dinner by a handsome man. There was no question or hesitation, I said yes.

The club was closing, and as we all got up to leave, I realised I was stuck. My arm that was nonchalantly hanging over the back of the couch had somehow gotten stuck between the wall and the wall heater. Everyone gathered around and had a go pulling me out. After pulling, twisting, turning and a little bit of bruising it finally came unstuck and I was able to make my escape, slinking out the club with much embarrassment.

Denz still showed up the next day and we went out for

BERLIN PART 2

dinner and drinks. It was honestly so refreshing to pretend that I didn't have a past and that the present moment was all there was. I could relax and just simply enjoy myself, enjoy the companionship without it being heavy and loaded with meaning. Up until that point I had never experienced that. Whenever I have been in the presence of someone I find attractive, I fall to pieces wondering if they like me and if there is any future between us. It's just so exhausting!

There we both were, lounging on the banquette in a low-lit bar after dinner, Denz with his smattering of English and me with my non-existent German. It must have been confusing for him not understanding how I was feeling as I didn't have the words to give to him. He didn't know my story so he saw my enjoyment of the moment as something more. He thought that I was into him and wanted a relationship. Which in his halting English, I could tell he didn't want.

As Denz liked a spliff or two, pulling one out of his pocket ready to go, we got stoned, thinking this would enhance our senses so we could understand each other. We decided that we would just tell each other how we feel and see if we could make sense of it. I understood him, as his English was so much better than my version of his language. I did try to get the bartender to help but I'm not sure how much was lost in translation. Nevertheless, we parted as friends with a kiss and a hug.

    I am not sure if he will ever know what a reprieve he gave me. He interrupted the never-ending onslaught of hopelessness and gifted me with the space to just be, to feel cared for, to feel as though I was beautiful and interesting.

    Those interludes in my last days in Berlin, after my brush with suicide, were lifesaving. They gave me the strength to keep going. But I was tired of being on my own. I wanted someone's support to get through the day and I just wanted to go home. There was still one more week to go so I pushed the fatigue aside and headed off to New York.

CHAPTER 10

New York

I feel embarrassed to say this, especially as everyone always raves about how amazing the city that never sleeps is, but I never gave New York a chance. I squandered my time there as I just wanted to come home, I wanted to be around my friends. I was sick of having to navigate my existence around the world.

    I stayed in a youth hostel on the Upper West Side instead of a hotel as funds were getting a bit low. I tried to get the momentum going and ticked off my tourist duties. I walked through nearby Central Park, went on a boat tour around Manhattan and got a glimpse of the majestic Statue of Liberty, saw a few museums and art galleries, then got depressed and hid in my room for a day or two.

UNTANGLED

I suppose I should be grateful that it wasn't another full-blown tsunami. There were still lots of tears but to a lesser degree. It seemed that Tokyo and Berlin had washed out a lot of the intensity.

By this stage, my white-blonde hair had turned an interesting shade of yellow and was ratty with frizzy ends. I was also sick of looking like a sad ghost! Vanity is a motivating factor and helped pick me off the floor, shower, get dressed and go and find the nearest hairdressers.

I found what looked a very pedestrian salon. Thank goodness I only wanted to go back to my natural hair colour. They certainly looked like they might specialise in mousy brown (although my mother insists that my hair is golden blonde), so it should have been safe and not too expensive.

My hairdresser was totally uninterested in me and my story. I didn't take it personally as I think he felt that way about all humankind. We both made token efforts at small talk but very soon fell blissfully silent while he layered my hair in brown dye and alfoil. After a couple of hours my hair was back to normal. The ghost was gone, and I looked like a human again. Who would have thought that mousy brown could bring back some colour and life.

But when my hairdresser presented me with the bill, I

NEW YORK

nearly choked! It was over AU$600 and that was in 2007! Why on earth didn't I ask how much it would be before I sat down? Luckily, I had transferred some money into my account the night before so I could cover the cost of the highway robbery (or hairway robbery!). But when they processed my credit card it was declined.

I could feel panic bubbling up and sweat building up on my brow. It was declined again! By this stage I was in a sheer state of terror. What was I going to do? I couldn't function. He suggested that maybe I go next door into the general store and try the ATM.

I found the ATM tucked away in the corner of the shop and started pounding away on the keys, willing my money to be there. But time after time I was declined. It seemed that my funds were still in transit out in cyberspace! By this time, I had shifted from panic, had gone past terror and was in such a state that I started alternating between blacking out and nausea. In the end, the blackout won as I faceplanted to the floor.

I came to splayed on the floor with people hovering around me. Concerned voices asked if I was diabetic and if I was on any medication. One man with a thick Bronx accent called me 'Mam' and let me know that my wallet was on the ground next to me. Their kindness and care were touching and something that I didn't expect to find, but then I didn't expect to pass out either! They helped me onto an overturned crate that I had knocked over on my way down to the ground. The owner of the store gave me a banana to help, which I accepted with as much dignity as I could possibly muster at the time.

So, there I was in New York City in an unknown general store on a milk crate eating a banana. No one knew I was here – no one would have believed me anyway – and I still didn't know what to do about the money for my hair. Oh my god! The hairdressers were still waiting on me and must have thought I'd done a runner! I went next door and told them what had happened, and yes, they were freaking out a bit. Surprisingly, they were understanding, and I left them with my Visa card to come back the next day to make the payment.

I thought about the kindness shown to me that day and recalled the kindnesses shown to me throughout my trip. I felt hopeful again. Maybe I am not on my own, abandoned in a hostile universe after all!

On my last night before going home, I took myself out for dinner to a jazz bar that my Lonely Planet had recommended. It was long and narrow with a stage at the far end with a sumptuous red velvet curtain as the backdrop, and little tables with dimly lit lamps on them (I love low lighting; everyone looks

NEW YORK

much more attractive). The bar was set up for dining and framed by two enormous chandeliers. They must have known that the bar is my go-to dining comfort space as that is exactly where they put me.

Greg the barman was tall and good-looking in a ginger kind of way and had a way of making you feel at ease straightaway with his easy, friendly manner. He seemed interested in everything I had to say, which makes him a consummate professional. That takes skill. We chatted while I ate, drank, watched the band and told him my life story, omitting the last 10 months, of course, as I didn't want to start crying at the bar! He shared with me that he and his wife were actors and were working in hospitality to support themselves and they'd just had a little baby girl. It was so lovely being a part of someone else's world. I felt like I was chatting to a friend.

Unbeknownst to me, there were two seatings for dinner. I didn't realise it but I had booked the earlier one. Greg had let me stay. What a legend! How kind. Buoyed by my newfound friendship with Greg and his kindness, I bought him and the band a round of drinks. And just like in Berlin and Tokyo, it ensured my popularity and for the third time on my trip, I had another lock in!

Greg and all the musicians stayed on with me and we continued drinking, laughing and telling stories. About this time, the handsome bass player, who had been flirting outrageously with me, leaned over and kissed me. I think he was super keen to continue it somewhere else but as I was a bit sideways and with a plane to catch later, I headed out into the night to try and sober up, walking back to the hostel.

As a car full of big, burly blokes pulled up at the lights opposite me, the thought did cross my mind, I'm not sure how safe it is to walk home drunk, late at night on your own as a woman in New York. The driver wound down his window and yelled at me, 'Get home safe, Gorgeous!', with a big smile on his face. 'Thanks, lovely, I will,' I yelled back with a wave. It appeared that New York was looking out for me to keep me safe until I got home!

CHAPTER 11

Untangling

Coming home was a mixed bag of lollies! It was so wonderful to be with my friends again and to be in my own bed, but I felt that I couldn't share with them what had happened over the few months I was away.

I felt like a failure because I had been in all these amazing cities and had just cried my way around the world. I hadn't found a new city to escape to, like I said I would, one where I was free and a success. I had dragged my literal and emotional baggage everywhere I had gone, and it had tainted all my experiences and wasted all my money. The lovely memories of fun, kindness and connection became overshadowed and then faded.

Life continued, rent had to be paid. I fell back into hospitality like a well-worn glove. Time passed and the depression rolled in! I finally sought the help that I had promised myself a year ago in Berlin.

When I walked into Dr Joan's practice, I was delighted to be met with an adorable, loving grandma. She was a wise, compassionate sage who gave me a glimpse into the window of my past and helped me see how everything that had happened to me was connected.

In our first session, I fully expected to be talking about Stuart as that's what I was depressed about, right? But instead, we started talking about my mother and father and how the complications of those formative relationships had led to getting stuck in the grieving process. I had never heard of complicated grief before. There is something freeing when you can put a label to what you are feeling.

Being stuck in complicated grief explained why I was having such intense ebb and flow loops. When I got to a certain point and the grief naturally wanted to be expressed, I would be overwhelmed by these emotions and shut them down until the next time they would try and be expressed again. If I had just allowed the intensity of the emotion to run its course, I would have eventually found relief quite naturally. But because I had

UNTANGLING

shut them down, my emotions had never had the chance to lose their intensity.

Dr Joan's sessions were an eye-opener for me and a herald of my journey to begin untangling my past and to find the authentic me underneath the hot mess.

I began a decade-long re-education of myself. I learnt how to be a film special effects make-up artist and had a go at working in film and TV. I then decided that I would become a theatre set designer and did my degree in theatre production and worked in theatre, and then as a set stylist in the events industry. I've worked as an usher at the Arts Centre Melbourne, then became a reiki master practitioner, a life coach and also an art teacher, running life drawing classes. I read any self-help book that came my way and attended any self-help course that resonated with me for where I was at the time. I built up my emotional intelligence and energetic awareness.

From having these different experiences and learning not to be so scared to try something new, I started to see through all the layers that I had built up around me to keep me safe. I saw the dysfunctional patterns I had been playing out from a young age. I could finally see the truth of what Dr Joan had tried to show me.

It's funny how sometimes you think you can't remember

moments from when you were very young. But if you slow down and focus you can see every emotion has been preserved in the body and when you tune into that feeling in your body then up comes that memory.

I remember the feeling in my body as an 18-month-old when my dad left and never came back. Well, he did about three years later but at the time it felt like he had died. It felt like he had abandoned me. I felt the despair of him never coming back. He had forgotten me, and I felt powerless because I couldn't change anything. I decided that there must be something wrong with me. I must be the reason why he left.

A year after dad left, my younger brother died in a car accident. I was almost three years old, and he had just turned one. I felt responsible for his death. I think I felt bad because I was so jealous of him as he got all Mum's attention and he got to sit on her lap when we had a family photo done. I was mad at him and then he died. It was my fault.

My mum, understandably, was a wreck and there was a point when, for her own sanity, she needed to go away. She went overseas for eight weeks. I guess just like me she wanted to run away from her life, to escape that terrible pain. As a three-year-old, I certainly didn't have the capacity to understand the complexity of her feelings, I could only feel my own. I remember

UNTANGLING

clearly, a few weeks into my stay with the babysitter, this feeling of total despair and abandonment. My father, my brother and now my mother have left me and I am totally alone. No one wants me. I am powerless to stop this. There must be something wrong with me.

I had made all these assumptions about myself and my world at such a young age, as we all do, and had set up a dysfunctional structure for my life. It was reinforced in my mum's second marriage. My stepfather was a sadistic, weak man who took great pleasure in physically and mentally abusing me behind my mum's back. It just proved to me again that I was on my own, I was powerless and there was something wrong with me.

So, when Stuart died the same old despair and beliefs came bubbling up. Everyone leaves me because there is something wrong with me. He died and it's my fault. I am alone and abandoned. No wonder I couldn't grieve naturally! I was overburdened with these insidious beliefs.

When I look at my time overseas, I see the same beliefs creating the patterns of my experience. I created experiences to validate the belief of abandonment and of being alone. I was that little three-year-old, despairing girl lost in the Japanese forest, wandering the streets of Berlin, terrified in the general store in New York. It was only when these were interrupted that I had the space to experience those moments of connection.

Stuart changed me. He gifted me the opportunity to clearly see the destructive patterns that had been running the show and I've had the chance to transform them from one of the worst experiences in my life into a life that has freedom and variety.

CHAPTER 12

Final musings

It has been so healing writing my story and sharing it with you. It has allowed me to go back and look at this wounding and find the truth, which is so much easier to identify in hindsight. I have the advantage of the distance of time to go back into these memories and it has allowed me the chance to have more compassion, empathy and forgiveness for who I was back then and to see the depth of the complexity that I was dealing with.

At the time, my perception was clouded by a powerful sense of rejection, betrayal and feelings of failure that I wasn't enough to save Stuart. I was defining him by his illness and his actions in his final years. I was defining myself as powerless and alone. I have felt shame that I disassociated from Stuart's death.

UNTANGLED

I have seen myself as weak for getting caught up in the complicated grief loop, being so overwhelmed by grief that I can't get to the other side because I had shut myself off. For keeping myself safe and small and caught up in the lack cycle because I felt like I didn't deserve any better. I have been ashamed of me.

But that 35-year-old past version of me had absolutely no idea what to do or how to be because I had no internal resources to draw from and no way to support myself through that minefield. I had never experienced anything like this before, or since. I was floundering in a barren landscape knowing no one who had walked that same path. I was doing the very best that I knew how to do at the time. I couldn't have made choices other than the ones that I did, and those choices have sculpted the person that I have become.

Allowing myself to see this clearly, I now feel a bit in awe of that younger version of me. She was the one who went into that mess emotionally unaware and unprepared. I feel such compassion and love for her courage and wish I could go back in time and just give younger me a big hug. I feel I can finally forgive myself, but then I realise there is nothing to forgive myself for.

I have been writing to you, my dear friend, as another version of me. The version that is 17 years older, that under-

FINAL MUSINGS

stands the energetic and emotional world as a reiki healer, that is in a loving supportive partnership with a new love. I am the version of me now that has the internal resources to experience grief consciously, honestly and gracefully and I have since done so.

As you navigate your way through your own hot mess and begin untangling the knots in your own life, I ask you to be kind to yourself. Claim your space, listen to yourself. Cry and wail no matter who is in front of you. Don't think you have to make it ok for everyone at the cost of yourself. Let the grief bubble up when it needs to and honour it for 'This too shall pass'. You need to follow your own path and grieve your own way. You might not feel that you've got this, but you have. Everything you do is absolutely perfect for you and chosen with the absolute best of what you know right now. Trust yourself. You are laying the groundwork for a richer, more loving, compassionate you.

May you see the beauty in your experience.

You've got this!

With much love,

Alexandra

ACKNOWLEDGEMENTS

Craig Boyes, my beautiful partner, without whose love and support this book might never have been expressed.

Nerina Lascelles, who has grieved with grace and integrity, honouring her sister Kate's passing. She inspired me to have the courage to revisit mine.

Amrik Singh, a wonderful, wise and compassionate soul. A true friend indeed.

Wendy, my mother, a strong, vibrant, vivacious woman who has endured much and whose strength inspires me.

William Whitecloud's Natural Success curriculum, for giving me techniques to separate myself from my wound and truly follow my heart.

ACKNOWLEDGEMENTS

Alex Blake, for showing me how to access my untold story.

Casey Cheah, my Reiki Master teacher, who showed me a whole new world of energy and healing.

And to the many others who were there and supported me, I am eternally grateful.

ABOUT THE AUTHOR

Alexandra has collected and excelled at her many passions over the years, but at her heart she is, and always will be, an artist.

With a bachelor's degree in both fine arts and production in the dramatic arts, writing is now her newfound expression.

In addition to her visual art and writing, Alexandra is a practising Reiki Master. She lives in Melbourne with her partner, nieces and rescue pets.

www.ingramcontent.com/pod-product-compliance
Lightning Source LLC
Chambersburg PA
CBHW062041290426
44109CB00026B/2699